IMAGINE THAT!!!

Exploring
Make-Believe

by Joyce Strauss

illustrations by Jennifer Barrett

HUMAN SCIENCES PRESS, INC.
72 FIFTH AVENUE
NEW YORK, N.Y. 10011

Printed in the United States of America
Published by Human Sciences Press, Inc.
72 5th Ave. New York, NY 10011

Strauss, Joyce 1936-
   Imagine that!!!

   SUMMARY: Describes a variety of situations and in-
cludes questions intended to stimulate the imagination.
   1. Imagination—Problems, exercises, etc.—Juve-
nile literature. [1. Imagination] I. Barrett, Jennifer, ill.
II. Title.
BF408.S824   153.3   82-1089
ISBN 0-89885-128-9   AACR2

My deep appreciation to
Dr. Joseph Shorr, author of
"Go See the Movie in Your Head"
and *Psychotherapy Through
Imagery*, second edition. His
class in imagery, which
I participated in, stimulated
my own imagination to
create this book.

This book is dedicated to
that part in all of us which believes
that anything is possible.

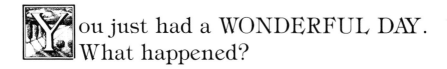ou just had a WONDERFUL DAY.
What happened?

If you had a MAGIC CARPET that would take you anywhere you wanted to go, where would you go? What would it be like?

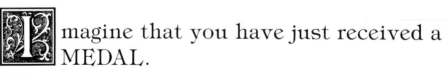

magine that you have just received a
MEDAL.
What was it given to you for?

If you could change yourself into SOMETHING ELSE, what would it be? What would it do?

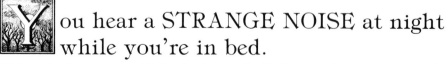ou hear a STRANGE NOISE at night
while you're in bed.
What do you think it is? What do you do?

reate someone your same age.
Describe what that person is like.
What could you do together?

f a flower began TALKING to you,
what do you think it would say?

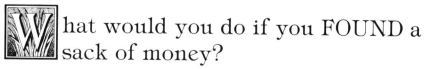 hat would you do if you FOUND a sack of money?

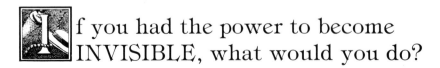f you had the power to become INVISIBLE, what would you do?

You've just written a SHORT STORY. What is it about?

You are FIFTY years older than you are right now. What are you like? What do you like to do?

ou have a garden and can GROW anything you want to.
I have chosen to grow a horse, a tree, and a bench. What do you choose to grow?

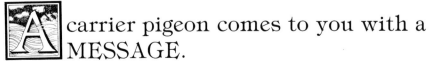 carrier pigeon comes to you with a
MESSAGE.
Who is it from? What does it say?

Your hand has turned into a MAGIC
WAND and you can change anything
into whatever you want just by tapping
your fingers. What do you change?

n the ground there is a KEY. Behind the key are many doors, each door different from the next. Which door would you open? What would you find?

ou're in the ocean and a DOLPHIN
offers you a ride and you accept.
Where do you go? What do you see?

ct out what you would do if you found out that you had just turned into . . .

. . . a CLOWN? . . . a TEACHER? . . . a BUS DRIVER? . . . a FARMER? . . . a POLICE OFFICER?

omeone that you have never met
gives you a GIFT.
What is it? Why do you think they gave it
to you?

retend you could do ANYTHING you want to.
What do you do?

What would you do if YOUR ARMS became wings and you could fly?

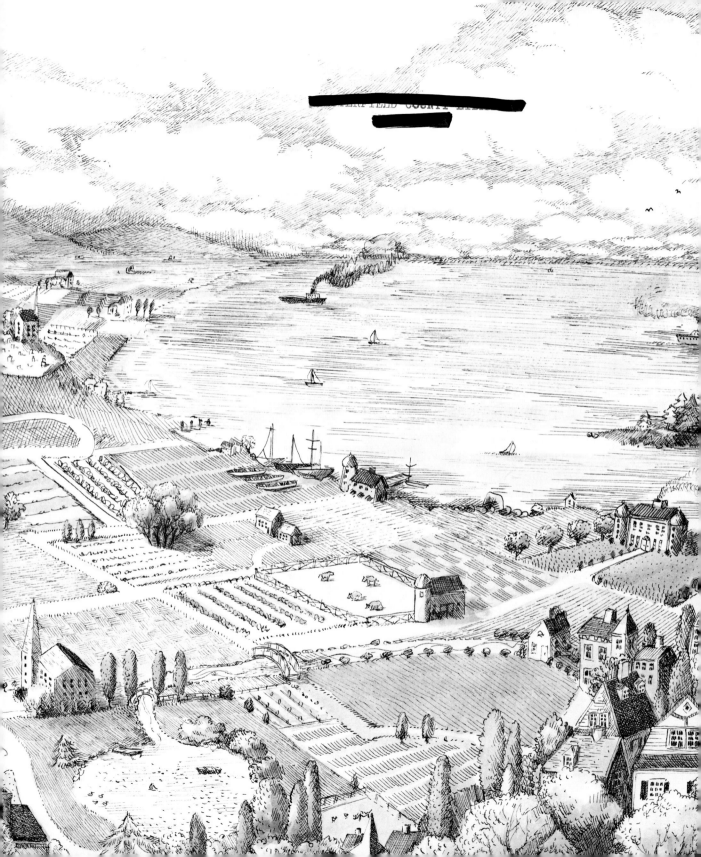

What would you do if you received a
free TICKET to an enchanted island?
If you went to it, describe what it would be
like.

f you found a BOX and you opened
the lid, what would you find inside?

Describe what you would do if you
BECAME a . . . BUTTERFLY? . . .
MONKEY? . . . BALL? . . . TREE? . . .
ROCK? . . . SNAKE?

What would it be like if you had EVERYTHING you ever wanted?

I magine you could write a BOOK just
like this book.
What would some of the questions be?